D1795478

The Runner's Success Journal
Transform Your Mindset in 90 Days

Authors: Michelle Griffiths-Reeve and Jo Outram

Copyright © 2021 by Jo Outram.

All rights reserved. This book or any portion thereof may not be reproduced or used in any manner whatsoever without the express permission of the publisher or author except for the use of brief quotations in a book review or scholarly journal.

The published makes no representation, expressed or implied, with regards to the accuracy of the information contained in this book, and cannot accept any responsibility or liability. The comments made do not constitute professional advice.

First Printing: 2021

ISBN: 9 7 8 - 1 - 6 6 7 1 - 8 8 2 0 - 1

Printed in the UK

The Runner's Success Journal

Congratulations for purchasing the runner's success journal. This is the first step in your journey to training and competing with confidence! Jo and I are so excited to be with you as you move towards running at your best!

Success in running is underpinned by self-belief and confidence, and just a few tweaks in your mindset can help you move forward and achieve your dreams, both in your running and in your life. Having used Jo's method myself, as well as with my clients, I want to share the benefits with you.

Affirmations are an extremely powerful tool in sport. Used regularly, they prime your brain for better performance. To improve your running mindset, you need to start re-programming your underlying belief system to allow you to believe that you are capable of achieving what you desire. Our beliefs drive our self-talk, something that is central to our mindset. Negative self-talk can hold you back, with old, untrue stories hindering you from moving out of your comfort zone and towards your best.

The good news is that you can re-program your beliefs and mindset by getting clear on what you want to achieve; quietening the negative chatter in your brain; clearing the negative beliefs; and then replacing them with positive ones (affirmations).

Follow the steps that we've laid out for you and try to complete the journal each day. Don't worry if you miss a day, just get back into the process as soon as you can - and keep moving forward.

It's time for you to run, train and compete at your best!

Michelle x

I'm delighted to share with you my five-step process for using affirmations and the Law of Attraction to help improve your mindset, your confidence and your ability to become a better runner.

You might have used the Law of Attraction before, with mixed or no results. If this is you, then know that you are not alone. I've been there and so have many of my clients before they started using this system. The main problem for the lack of results is that most people just ask, without being specific, and then give up when they do not receive!

First, the Law of Attraction does not always give results straight away. Giving up just cancels your order as the Universe thinks you no longer want what you have asked for. It is also difficult to manifest when you are coming from a place of desperation and don't belief in yourself.

Doubts are a big problem. These doubts (also referred to as limiting beliefs or blocks) are often buried in our unconscious mind. This is a problem as we act on these negative beliefs without even knowing we are doing this.

Follow the steps that we have included in the following pages and you'll be able to start using affirmations and the Law of Attraction to improve your mindset and start building the life you deserve. Yes, it's true: you really do deserve to be the runner that you desire to be.

Jo x

Step 1

You need to get super clear and specific about what you want to achieve in your running career, plus the things you don't want. You'll need to take some time to do this.

Find some quiet time, make yourself a drink, close the door, switch off all electronic distractions - and think. You may want to meditate. A simple meditation will suffice.

Sit comfortably. You don't have to sit on the floor in the lotus position, unless you are flexible enough for this to be comfortable. Sit in a comfortable chair if you prefer but sit without crossing your legs.

Close your eyes when it feels right to do so. Focus on your breathing by becoming aware of your abdomen as you breathe in and out. Just breathe normally.

Then when you feel ready, start to think about:

➢ What does success in running mean to you?

➢ What does it feel like?

➢ Think about your ideal performance: where are you, who are you with, what are you aiming for?

➢ What will you get from this ideal performance?

Then when you are ready, open your eyes and use the journal to note and work through the thoughts you have had. You might want to do this exercise several times until you are happy that you have captured all your thoughts.

Step 2

You are going to use positive affirmations to reinforce what you need to believe in order to convince yourself that you are a worthy and capable runner.

Affirmations are words or phrases which you say repeatedly to affirm a thought about yourself. Thoughts that are repeated often enough soon become beliefs.

Each day you should choose an affirmation to work with. Try to work through the process every day, but if you miss a day, don't beat yourself up, or even worse, give up. Just continue where you left off.

Some affirmations have been included in this journal but feel free to write your own, or to adjust them to make them specific to your running goal or event. If you do write your own, just make sure that you write them in the present tense, and, of course, that they are positive.

To use the ones provided here, just scan through the list (at the back of the journal) each day. When you read one that resonates with you, that's the one you need to work with for that day. If you are drawn to an affirmation, but instantly conclude, for whatever reason, that it is not right for you, then it is probably a good idea to choose this one, in order that you can work on dispelling the negativity it conjures up.

There are more than enough affirmations to cover all 90 days, but if you are drawn to an affirmation that you have used before, then use it again. It does not matter if you use an affirmation more than once.

Write your affirmation in the box provided for each day. Write it out several times and say it to yourself in your head or out loud.

You need to do what makes you feel comfortable at the start of the 90 days. When you are ready, you can say the affirmation out loud whilst looking at yourself in the mirror. When you do this, aim to stand upright in a strong, confident pose, one that a confident athlete would hold. Only do this when you feel ready to do so. By the end of 90 days, you should be getting comfortable enough to do this.

As you get more comfortable with the affirmations you may find you want to use certain ones outside of this journal, when you're training, or competing. While there is no requirement to do this, you are welcome to use the affirmations during a run in whatever way you feel is natural and beneficial.

Step 3

If you start to doubt the affirmations that you have chosen, do not worry, it is just your unconscious mind sending a signal which is based on your current belief system. You do, however, need to work on getting rid of these doubts, negative beliefs, or blocks.

Each day, when you are writing and saying your affirmation, take notice of any negative beliefs or doubts that you have and make a note of these in the journal. Space has been provided for you to do this. If you don't have any doubts, then that's great - there is less work to do on that day!

Do you have doubts right now about not being able to succeed as a runner? If you do, then get them out into the open. We've left some space for you here to write them down. Recognising and acknowledging doubts will empower you to work through them.

....

....

....

....

....

....

....

....

....

....

....

....

Step 4

You need to work on clearing your negative beliefs. If you don't, they'll undermine your confidence in your positive affirmations. Ultimately, they'll reduce your ability to run with confidence, and at your best.

There are several ways you can work on clearing your negative beliefs, including using methods like CBT and EMDR, which can be very effective, although they lie outside the scope of this journal.

However, the method that you will employ in this journal is the ancient Hawaiian mantra called *Ho'oponopono*. The Ho'oponopono has a long history, and many millions of people are convinced of its power to transform lives. There is even a fascinating story of how an Hawaiian Doctor claimed to have cured a whole ward of mentally ill criminals using Ho'oponopono - and he did not even visit any of the patients! If you are intrigued to learn more, we wholeheartedly recommend the book *Zero Limits* by Dr Joe Vitale.

The mantra is simply the following four phrases.

I'm sorry

Please forgive me

Thank you

I love you

I'm sorry. This is our repentance. According to the Law of Attraction, we are responsible for what our mind attracts to us, because we attract it, albeit on a unconscious level. Once you can accept this then it becomes very natural to feel sorry.

Please forgive me. You need to say this and mean it. It does not matter who you are asking forgiveness from, whether it is yourself, the Universe, or God. But note: you are not asking forgiveness from another person. You do not need their forgiveness.

Thank You. This is a show of gratitude. Again, it does not matter who you are saying it to – yourself, the Universe, God. Just say it with feeling.

I love you. Again it does not matter to whom, or what, you address these words. But be sure they come from the heart.

You can say these phrases in any order.

Whether you regard the Ho'oponopono in a spiritual context, or see it rather as a practical tool, is, of course, an entirely personal matter. What is important is that it is known to possess transformative powers, enabling you to move beyond the negative self-beliefs you might encounter when beginning your affirmations practice.

You are going to use this mantra each day, by taking each doubt or negative belief in turn, and saying the prayer several times. You can say the mantra to yourself anytime of the day, even without knowing what sort of negative feelings you want to clear.

Step 5

Finally, we are going to show gratitude.

If you are not doing so already, then a good habit to develop is gratitude for what you already have. Research has shown that writing down what we are grateful for has resulted in some impressive benefits, including peak performance!

You should not, however, just go through the motions. You must make a conscious decision to become more grateful - for the things around you, for the people in your life, and the unexpected events. When writing what you are grateful for, you should try to use as much detail as possible. For example, "I am grateful for the support I received from my family today, helping me deal with the problems I was having at work" is more meaningful than just "I am grateful for my family."

One word of advice: be careful when recording the things that you are grateful for that you don't overdo it. Recording gratitudes mechanically day-in-day-out can inevitably dilute the strength of the feelings that first gave rise to them, until potentially we forget that we really *are* grateful. So, if you feel that writing daily isn't for you, that's fine: so long as you are writing regularly. This might be every other day, or a few times a week. Whatever works for you.

Welcome to the beginning of your journey

The Runner's Success Journal
Transform Your Mindset in 90 Days

Day 1

Today's Affirmation:

Say this affirmation several times out loud with your hand on your heart looking at yourself in the mirror.

If you prefer to write it down, do that here.

1. ....
2. ....
3. ....
4. ....
5. ....

Date:

How does this affirmation make you feel?

....

....

....

....

What blocks/negative beliefs are brought up for you

....

....

....

....

Thinking of each block in turn, now say:

- *Please forgive me*
- *I'm sorry*
- *Thank you*
- *I love you*

Today I am grateful for:

....

....

....

Day 2

Today's Affirmation:

Say this affirmation several times out loud with your hand on your heart looking at yourself in the mirror.

If you prefer to write it down, do that here.

1. ....
2. ....
3. ....
4. ....
5. ....

Date:

How does this affirmation make you feel?

....

....

....

....

What blocks/negative beliefs are brought up for you

....

....

....

....

Thinking of each block in turn, now say:

- *Please forgive me*
- *I'm sorry*
- *Thank you*
- *I love you*

Today I am grateful for:

....

....

....

Day 3

Today's Affirmation:

Say this affirmation several times out loud with your hand on your heart looking at yourself in the mirror.

If you prefer to write it down, do that here.

1. ....
2. ....
3. ....
4. ....
5. ....

Date:

How does this affirmation make you feel?

....

....

....

....

What blocks/negative beliefs are brought up for you

....

....

....

....

Thinking of each block in turn, now say:

- *Please forgive me*
- *I'm sorry*
- *Thank you*
- *I love you*

Today I am grateful for:

....

....

....

Day 4

Today's Affirmation:

Say this affirmation several times out loud with your hand on your heart looking at yourself in the mirror.

If you prefer to write it down, do that here.

1. ....
2. ....
3. ....
4. ....
5. ....

Date:

How does this affirmation make you feel?

....
....
....
....

What blocks/negative beliefs are brought up for you

....
....
....
....

Thinking of each block in turn, now say:

- *Please forgive me*
- *I'm sorry*
- *Thank you*
- *I love you*

Today I am grateful for:

....
....
....

Day 5

Today's Affirmation:

Say this affirmation several times out loud with your hand on your heart looking at yourself in the mirror.

If you prefer to write it down, do that here.

1. ....
2. ....
3. ....
4. ....
5. ....

Date:

How does this affirmation make you feel?

....

....

....

....

What blocks/negative beliefs are brought up for you

....

....

....

....

Thinking of each block in turn, now say:

- *Please forgive me*
- *I'm sorry*
- *Thank you*
- *I love you*

Today I am grateful for:

....

....

....

Day 6

Today's Affirmation:

Say this affirmation several times out loud with your hand on your heart looking at yourself in the mirror.

If you prefer to write it down, do that here.

1. ....
2. ....
3. ....
4. ....
5. ....

Date:

How does this affirmation make you feel?

....

....

....

....

What blocks/negative beliefs are brought up for you

....

....

....

....

Thinking of each block in turn, now say:

- *Please forgive me*
- *I'm sorry*
- *Thank you*
- *I love you*

Today I am grateful for:

....

....

....

Day 7

Today's Affirmation:

Say this affirmation several times out loud with your hand on your heart looking at yourself in the mirror.

If you prefer to write it down, do that here.

1. ....

2. ....

3. ....

4. ....

5. ....

Date:

How does this affirmation make you feel?

....

....

....

....

What blocks/negative beliefs are brought up for you

....

....

....

....

Thinking of each block in turn, now say:

- *Please forgive me*
- *I'm sorry*
- *Thank you*
- *I love you*

Today I am grateful for:

....

....

....

Day 8

Today's Affirmation:

Say this affirmation several times out loud with your hand on your heart looking at yourself in the mirror.

If you prefer to write it down, do that here.

1. ....
2. ....
3. ....
4. ....
5. ....

Date:

How does this affirmation make you feel?

....

....

....

....

What blocks/negative beliefs are brought up for you

....

....

....

....

Thinking of each block in turn, now say:

- *Please forgive me*
- *I'm sorry*
- *Thank you*
- *I love you*

Today I am grateful for:

....

....

....

Day 9

Today's Affirmation:

Say this affirmation several times out loud with your hand on your heart looking at yourself in the mirror.

If you prefer to write it down, do that here.

1. ....
2. ....
3. ....
4. ....
5. ....

Date:

How does this affirmation make you feel?

....

....

....

....

What blocks/negative beliefs are brought up for you

....

....

....

....

Thinking of each block in turn, now say:

- *Please forgive me*
- *I'm sorry*
- *Thank you*
- *I love you*

Today I am grateful for:

....

....

....

Day 10

Today's Affirmation:

Say this affirmation several times out loud with your hand on your heart looking at yourself in the mirror.

If you prefer to write it down, do that here.

1. ....

2. ....

3. ....

4. ....

5. ....

Date:

How does this affirmation make you feel?

....

....

....

....

What blocks/negative beliefs are brought up for you

....

....

....

....

Thinking of each block in turn, now say:

- *Please forgive me*
- *I'm sorry*
- *Thank you*
- *I love you*

Today I am grateful for:

....

....

....

Day 11

Today's Affirmation:

Say this affirmation several times out loud with your hand on your heart looking at yourself in the mirror.

If you prefer to write it down, do that here.

1. ....
2. ....
3. ....
4. ....
5. ....

Date:

How does this affirmation make you feel?

....

....

....

....

What blocks/negative beliefs are brought up for you

....

....

....

....

Thinking of each block in turn, now say:

- *Please forgive me*
- *I'm sorry*
- *Thank you*
- *I love you*

Today I am grateful for:

....

....

....

Day 12

Today's Affirmation:

Say this affirmation several times out loud with your hand on your heart looking at yourself in the mirror.

If you prefer to write it down, do that here.

1. ....
2. ....
3. ....
4. ....
5. ....

Date:

How does this affirmation make you feel?

....

....

....

....

What blocks/negative beliefs are brought up for you

....

....

....

....

Thinking of each block in turn, now say:

- *Please forgive me*
- *I'm sorry*
- *Thank you*
- *I love you*

Today I am grateful for:

....

....

....

Day 13

Today's Affirmation:

Say this affirmation several times out loud with your hand on your heart looking at yourself in the mirror.

If you prefer to write it down, do that here.

1. ....
2. ....
3. ....
4. ....
5. ....

Date:

How does this affirmation make you feel?

....

....

....

....

What blocks/negative beliefs are brought up for you

....

....

....

....

Thinking of each block in turn, now say:

- *Please forgive me*
- *I'm sorry*
- *Thank you*
- *I love you*

Today I am grateful for:

....

....

....

Day 14

Today's Affirmation:

Say this affirmation several times out loud with your hand on your heart looking at yourself in the mirror.

If you prefer to write it down, do that here.

1. ....

2. ....

3. ....

4. ....

5. ....

Date:

How does this affirmation make you feel?

....

....

....

....

What blocks/negative beliefs are brought up for you

....

....

....

....

Thinking of each block in turn, now say:

- *Please forgive me*
- *I'm sorry*
- *Thank you*
- *I love you*

Today I am grateful for:

....

....

....

Day 15

Today's Affirmation:

Say this affirmation several times out loud with your hand on your heart looking at yourself in the mirror.

If you prefer to write it down, do that here.

1. ....
2. ....
3. ....
4. ....
5. ....

Date:

How does this affirmation make you feel?

....

....

....

....

What blocks/negative beliefs are brought up for you

....

....

....

....

Thinking of each block in turn, now say:

- *Please forgive me*
- *I'm sorry*
- *Thank you*
- *I love you*

Today I am grateful for:

....

....

....

Day 16

Today's Affirmation:

Say this affirmation several times out loud with your hand on your heart looking at yourself in the mirror.

If you prefer to write it down, do that here.

1. ....

2. ....

3. ....

4. ....

5. ....

Date:

How does this affirmation make you feel?

....

....

....

....

What blocks/negative beliefs are brought up for you

....

....

....

....

Thinking of each block in turn, now say:

- *Please forgive me*
- *I'm sorry*
- *Thank you*
- *I love you*

Today I am grateful for:

....

....

....

Day 17

Today's Affirmation:

Say this affirmation several times out loud with your hand on your heart looking at yourself in the mirror.

If you prefer to write it down, do that here.

1. ....
2. ....
3. ....
4. ....
5. ....

Date:

How does this affirmation make you feel?

....

....

....

....

What blocks/negative beliefs are brought up for you

....

....

....

....

Thinking of each block in turn, now say:

- *Please forgive me*
- *I'm sorry*
- *Thank you*
- *I love you*

Today I am grateful for:

....

....

....

Day 18

Today's Affirmation:

Say this affirmation several times out loud with your hand on your heart looking at yourself in the mirror.

If you prefer to write it down, do that here.

1. ....
2. ....
3. ....
4. ....
5. ....

Date:

How does this affirmation make you feel?

....
....
....
....

What blocks/negative beliefs are brought up for you

....
....
....
....

Thinking of each block in turn, now say:

- *Please forgive me*
- *I'm sorry*
- *Thank you*
- *I love you*

Today I am grateful for:

....
....
....

Day 19

Today's Affirmation:

Say this affirmation several times out loud with your hand on your heart looking at yourself in the mirror.

If you prefer to write it down, do that here.

1. ....
2. ....
3. ....
4. ....
5. ....

Date:

How does this affirmation make you feel?

....

....

....

....

What blocks/negative beliefs are brought up for you

....

....

....

....

Thinking of each block in turn, now say:

- *Please forgive me*
- *I'm sorry*
- *Thank you*
- *I love you*

Today I am grateful for:

....

....

....

Day 20

Today's Affirmation:

Say this affirmation several times out loud with your hand on your heart looking at yourself in the mirror.

If you prefer to write it down, do that here.

1. ....
2. ....
3. ....
4. ....
5. ....

Date:

How does this affirmation make you feel?

....

....

....

....

What blocks/negative beliefs are brought up for you

....

....

....

....

Thinking of each block in turn, now say:

- *Please forgive me*
- *I'm sorry*
- *Thank you*
- *I love you*

Today I am grateful for:

....

....

....

Day 21

Today's Affirmation:

Say this affirmation several times out loud with your hand on your heart looking at yourself in the mirror.

If you prefer to write it down, do that here.

1. ....
2. ....
3. ....
4. ....
5. ....

Date:

How does this affirmation make you feel?

....

....

....

....

What blocks/negative beliefs are brought up for you

....

....

....

....

Thinking of each block in turn, now say:

- *Please forgive me*
- *I'm sorry*
- *Thank you*
- *I love you*

Today I am grateful for:

....

....

....

Day 22

Today's Affirmation:

Say this affirmation several times out loud with your hand on your heart looking at yourself in the mirror.

If you prefer to write it down, do that here.

1. ....
2. ....
3. ....
4. ....
5. ....

Date:

How does this affirmation make you feel?

....

....

....

....

What blocks/negative beliefs are brought up for you

....

....

....

....

Thinking of each block in turn, now say:

- *Please forgive me*
- *I'm sorry*
- *Thank you*
- *I love you*

Today I am grateful for:

....

....

....

Day 23

Today's Affirmation:

Say this affirmation several times out loud with your hand on your heart looking at yourself in the mirror.

If you prefer to write it down, do that here.

1. ....
2. ....
3. ....
4. ....
5. ....

Date:

How does this affirmation make you feel?

....

....

....

....

What blocks/negative beliefs are brought up for you

....

....

....

....

Thinking of each block in turn, now say:

- *Please forgive me*
- *I'm sorry*
- *Thank you*
- *I love you*

Today I am grateful for:

....

....

....

Day 24

Today's Affirmation:

Say this affirmation several times out loud with your hand on your heart looking at yourself in the mirror.

If you prefer to write it down, do that here.

1. ....
2. ....
3. ....
4. ....
5. ....

Date:

How does this affirmation make you feel?

....

....

....

....

What blocks/negative beliefs are brought up for you

....

....

....

....

Thinking of each block in turn, now say:

- *Please forgive me*
- *I'm sorry*
- *Thank you*
- *I love you*

Today I am grateful for:

....

....

....

Day 25

Today's Affirmation:

Say this affirmation several times out loud with your hand on your heart looking at yourself in the mirror.

If you prefer to write it down, do that here.

1. ....

2. ....

3. ....

4. ....

5. ....

Date:

How does this affirmation make you feel?

....
....
....
....

What blocks/negative beliefs are brought up for you

....
....
....
....

Thinking of each block in turn, now say:

- *Please forgive me*
- *I'm sorry*
- *Thank you*
- *I love you*

Today I am grateful for:

....
....
....

Day 26

Today's Affirmation:

Say this affirmation several times out loud with your hand on your heart looking at yourself in the mirror.

If you prefer to write it down, do that here.

1. ....
2. ....
3. ....
4. ....
5. ....

Date:

How does this affirmation make you feel?

....

....

....

....

What blocks/negative beliefs are brought up for you

....

....

....

....

Thinking of each block in turn, now say:

- *Please forgive me*
- *I'm sorry*
- *Thank you*
- *I love you*

Today I am grateful for:

....

....

....

Day 27

Today's Affirmation:

Say this affirmation several times out loud with your hand on your heart looking at yourself in the mirror.

If you prefer to write it down, do that here.

1. ....
2. ....
3. ....
4. ....
5. ....

Date:

How does this affirmation make you feel?

....

....

....

....

What blocks/negative beliefs are brought up for you

....

....

....

....

Thinking of each block in turn, now say:

- *Please forgive me*
- *I'm sorry*
- *Thank you*
- *I love you*

Today I am grateful for:

....

....

....

Day 28

Today's Affirmation:

Say this affirmation several times out loud with your hand on your heart looking at yourself in the mirror.

If you prefer to write it down, do that here.

1. ....
2. ....
3. ....
4. ....
5. ....

Date:

How does this affirmation make you feel?

....

....

....

....

What blocks/negative beliefs are brought up for you

....

....

....

....

Thinking of each block in turn, now say:

- *Please forgive me*
- *I'm sorry*
- *Thank you*
- *I love you*

Today I am grateful for:

....

....

....

Day 29

Today's Affirmation:

Say this affirmation several times out loud with your hand on your heart looking at yourself in the mirror.

If you prefer to write it down, do that here.

1. ....
2. ....
3. ....
4. ....
5. ....

Date:

How does this affirmation make you feel?

....

....

....

....

What blocks/negative beliefs are brought up for you

....

....

....

....

Thinking of each block in turn, now say:

- *Please forgive me*
- *I'm sorry*
- *Thank you*
- *I love you*

Today I am grateful for:

....

....

....

Day 30

Today's Affirmation:

Say this affirmation several times out loud with your hand on your heart looking at yourself in the mirror.

If you prefer to write it down, do that here.

1. ....
2. ....
3. ....
4. ....
5. ....

Date:

How does this affirmation make you feel?

....

....

....

....

What blocks/negative beliefs are brought up for you

....

....

....

....

Thinking of each block in turn, now say:

- *Please forgive me*
- *I'm sorry*
- *Thank you*
- *I love you*

Today I am grateful for:

....

....

....

How do I feel my mindset has improved over the last 30 days?

How do I want the Universe to guide me in the next 30 days?

Day 31

Today's Affirmation:

Say this affirmation several times out loud with your hand on your heart looking at yourself in the mirror.

If you prefer to write it down, do that here.

1. ....

2. ....

3. ....

4. ....

5. ....

Date:

How does this affirmation make you feel?

....

....

....

....

What blocks/negative beliefs are brought up for you

....

....

....

....

Thinking of each block in turn, now say:

- *Please forgive me*
- *I'm sorry*
- *Thank you*
- *I love you*

Today I am grateful for:

....

....

....

Day 32

Today's Affirmation:

Say this affirmation several times out loud with your hand on your heart looking at yourself in the mirror.

If you prefer to write it down, do that here.

1. ....

2. ....

3. ....

4. ....

5. ....

Date:

How does this affirmation make you feel?

....

....

....

....

What blocks/negative beliefs are brought up for you

....

....

....

....

Thinking of each block in turn, now say:

- *Please forgive me*
- *I'm sorry*
- *Thank you*
- *I love you*

Today I am grateful for:

....

....

....

Day 33

Today's Affirmation:

Say this affirmation several times out loud with your hand on your heart looking at yourself in the mirror.

If you prefer to write it down, do that here.

1. ....

2. ....

3. ....

4. ....

5. ....

Date:

How does this affirmation make you feel?

....

....

....

....

What blocks/negative beliefs are brought up for you

....

....

....

....

Thinking of each block in turn, now say:

- *Please forgive me*
- *I'm sorry*
- *Thank you*
- *I love you*

Today I am grateful for:

....

....

....

Day 34

Today's Affirmation:

Say this affirmation several times out loud with your hand on your heart looking at yourself in the mirror.

If you prefer to write it down, do that here.

1. ....
2. ....
3. ....
4. ....
5. ....

Date:

How does this affirmation make you feel?

....
....
....
....

What blocks/negative beliefs are brought up for you

....
....
....
....

Thinking of each block in turn, now say:

- *Please forgive me*
- *I'm sorry*
- *Thank you*
- *I love you*

Today I am grateful for:

....
....
....

Day 35

Today's Affirmation:

Say this affirmation several times out loud with your hand on your heart looking at yourself in the mirror.

If you prefer to write it down, do that here.

1. ....

2. ....

3. ....

4. ....

5. ....

Date:

How does this affirmation make you feel?

....
....
....
....

What blocks/negative beliefs are brought up for you

....
....
....
....

Thinking of each block in turn, now say:

- *Please forgive me*
- *I'm sorry*
- *Thank you*
- *I love you*

Today I am grateful for:

....
....
....

Day 36

Today's Affirmation:

Say this affirmation several times out loud with your hand on your heart looking at yourself in the mirror.

If you prefer to write it down, do that here.

1. ....
2. ....
3. ....
4. ....
5. ....

Date:

How does this affirmation make you feel?

....

....

....

....

What blocks/negative beliefs are brought up for you

....

....

....

....

Thinking of each block in turn, now say:

- *Please forgive me*
- *I'm sorry*
- *Thank you*
- *I love you*

Today I am grateful for:

....

....

....

Day 37

Today's Affirmation:

Say this affirmation several times out loud with your hand on your heart looking at yourself in the mirror.

If you prefer to write it down, do that here.

1. ....
2. ....
3. ....
4. ....
5. ....

Date:

How does this affirmation make you feel?

....
....
....
....

What blocks/negative beliefs are brought up for you

....
....
....
....

Thinking of each block in turn, now say:

- *Please forgive me*
- *I'm sorry*
- *Thank you*
- *I love you*

Today I am grateful for:

....
....
....

Day 38

Today's Affirmation:

Say this affirmation several times out loud with your hand on your heart looking at yourself in the mirror.

If you prefer to write it down, do that here.

1. ....
2. ....
3. ....
4. ....
5. ....

Date:

How does this affirmation make you feel?

....

....

....

....

What blocks/negative beliefs are brought up for you

....

....

....

....

Thinking of each block in turn, now say:

- *Please forgive me*
- *I'm sorry*
- *Thank you*
- *I love you*

Today I am grateful for:

....

....

....

Day 39

Today's Affirmation:

Say this affirmation several times out loud with your hand on your heart looking at yourself in the mirror.

If you prefer to write it down, do that here.

1. ....

2. ....

3. ....

4. ....

5. ....

Date:

How does this affirmation make you feel?

....

....

....

....

What blocks/negative beliefs are brought up for you

....

....

....

....

Thinking of each block in turn, now say:

- *Please forgive me*
- *I'm sorry*
- *Thank you*
- *I love you*

Today I am grateful for:

....

....

....

Day 40

Today's Affirmation:

Say this affirmation several times out loud with your hand on your heart looking at yourself in the mirror.

If you prefer to write it down, do that here.

1. ....
2. ....
3. ....
4. ....
5. ....

Date:

How does this affirmation make you feel?

....

....

....

....

What blocks/negative beliefs are brought up for you

....

....

....

....

Thinking of each block in turn, now say:

- *Please forgive me*
- *I'm sorry*
- *Thank you*
- *I love you*

Today I am grateful for:

....

....

....

Day 41

Today's Affirmation:

Say this affirmation several times out loud with your hand on your heart looking at yourself in the mirror.

If you prefer to write it down, do that here.

1. ....
2. ....
3. ....
4. ....
5. ....

Date:

How does this affirmation make you feel?

....
....
....
....

What blocks/negative beliefs are brought up for you

....
....
....
....

Thinking of each block in turn, now say:

- *Please forgive me*
- *I'm sorry*
- *Thank you*
- *I love you*

Today I am grateful for:

....
....
....

Day 42

Today's Affirmation:

Say this affirmation several times out loud with your hand on your heart looking at yourself in the mirror.

If you prefer to write it down, do that here.

1. ....
2. ....
3. ....
4. ....
5. ....

Date:

How does this affirmation make you feel?

....

....

....

....

What blocks/negative beliefs are brought up for you

....

....

....

....

Thinking of each block in turn, now say:

- *Please forgive me*
- *I'm sorry*
- *Thank you*
- *I love you*

Today I am grateful for:

....

....

....

Day 43

Today's Affirmation:

Say this affirmation several times out loud with your hand on your heart looking at yourself in the mirror.

If you prefer to write it down, do that here.

1. ....
2. ....
3. ....
4. ....
5. ....

Date:

How does this affirmation make you feel?

....

....

....

....

What blocks/negative beliefs are brought up for you

....

....

....

....

Thinking of each block in turn, now say:

- *Please forgive me*
- *I'm sorry*
- *Thank you*
- *I love you*

Today I am grateful for:

....

....

....

Day 44

Today's Affirmation:

Say this affirmation several times out loud with your hand on your heart looking at yourself in the mirror.

If you prefer to write it down, do that here.

1. ....
2. ....
3. ....
4. ....
5. ....

Date:

How does this affirmation make you feel?

....

....

....

....

What blocks/negative beliefs are brought up for you

....

....

....

....

Thinking of each block in turn, now say:

- *Please forgive me*
- *I'm sorry*
- *Thank you*
- *I love you*

Today I am grateful for:

....

....

....

Day 45

Today's Affirmation:

Say this affirmation several times out loud with your hand on your heart looking at yourself in the mirror.

If you prefer to write it down, do that here.

1. ....

2. ....

3. ....

4. ....

5. ....

Date:

How does this affirmation make you feel?

....

....

....

....

What blocks/negative beliefs are brought up for you

....

....

....

....

Thinking of each block in turn, now say:

- *Please forgive me*
- *I'm sorry*
- *Thank you*
- *I love you*

Today I am grateful for:

....

....

....

Day 46

Today's Affirmation:

Say this affirmation several times out loud with your hand on your heart looking at yourself in the mirror.

If you prefer to write it down, do that here.

1. ....

2. ....

3. ....

4. ....

5. ....

Date:

How does this affirmation make you feel?

....

....

....

....

What blocks/negative beliefs are brought up for you

....

....

....

....

Thinking of each block in turn, now say:

- *Please forgive me*
- *I'm sorry*
- *Thank you*
- *I love you*

Today I am grateful for:

....

....

....

Day 47

Today's Affirmation:

Say this affirmation several times out loud with your hand on your heart looking at yourself in the mirror.

If you prefer to write it down, do that here.

1. ....
2. ....
3. ....
4. ....
5. ....

Date:

How does this affirmation make you feel?

....
....
....
....

What blocks/negative beliefs are brought up for you

....
....
....
....

Thinking of each block in turn, now say:

- *Please forgive me*
- *I'm sorry*
- *Thank you*
- *I love you*

Today I am grateful for:

....
....
....

Day 48

Today's Affirmation:

Say this affirmation several times out loud with your hand on your heart looking at yourself in the mirror.

If you prefer to write it down, do that here.

1. ....
2. ....
3. ....
4. ....
5. ....

Date:

How does this affirmation make you feel?

....

....

....

....

What blocks/negative beliefs are brought up for you

....

....

....

....

Thinking of each block in turn, now say:

- *Please forgive me*
- *I'm sorry*
- *Thank you*
- *I love you*

Today I am grateful for:

....

....

....

Day 49

Today's Affirmation:

Say this affirmation several times out loud with your hand on your heart looking at yourself in the mirror.

If you prefer to write it down, do that here.

1. ....
2. ....
3. ....
4. ....
5. ....

Date:

How does this affirmation make you feel?

....

....

....

....

What blocks/negative beliefs are brought up for you

....

....

....

....

Thinking of each block in turn, now say:

- *Please forgive me*
- *I'm sorry*
- *Thank you*
- *I love you*

Today I am grateful for:

....

....

....

Day 50

Today's Affirmation:

Say this affirmation several times out loud with your hand on your heart looking at yourself in the mirror.

If you prefer to write it down, do that here.

1. ....
2. ....
3. ....
4. ....
5. ....

Date:

How does this affirmation make you feel?

....

....

....

....

What blocks/negative beliefs are brought up for you

....

....

....

....

Thinking of each block in turn, now say:

- *Please forgive me*
- *I'm sorry*
- *Thank you*
- *I love you*

Today I am grateful for:

....

....

....

Day 51

Today's Affirmation:

Say this affirmation several times out loud with your hand on your heart looking at yourself in the mirror.

If you prefer to write it down, do that here.

1. ....
2. ....
3. ....
4. ....
5. ....

Date:

How does this affirmation make you feel?

....

....

....

....

What blocks/negative beliefs are brought up for you

....

....

....

....

Thinking of each block in turn, now say:

- *Please forgive me*
- *I'm sorry*
- *Thank you*
- *I love you*

Today I am grateful for:

....

....

....

Day 52

Today's Affirmation:

Say this affirmation several times out loud with your hand on your heart looking at yourself in the mirror.

If you prefer to write it down, do that here.

1. ....
2. ....
3. ....
4. ....
5. ....

Date:

How does this affirmation make you feel?

....

....

....

....

What blocks/negative beliefs are brought up for you

....

....

....

....

Thinking of each block in turn, now say:

- *Please forgive me*
- *I'm sorry*
- *Thank you*
- *I love you*

Today I am grateful for:

....

....

....

Day 53

Today's Affirmation:

Say this affirmation several times out loud with your hand on your heart looking at yourself in the mirror.

If you prefer to write it down, do that here.

1. ....
2. ....
3. ....
4. ....
5. ....

Date:

How does this affirmation make you feel?

....

....

....

....

What blocks/negative beliefs are brought up for you

....

....

....

....

Thinking of each block in turn, now say:

- *Please forgive me*
- *I'm sorry*
- *Thank you*
- *I love you*

Today I am grateful for:

....

....

....

Day 54

Today's Affirmation:

Say this affirmation several times out loud with your hand on your heart looking at yourself in the mirror.

If you prefer to write it down, do that here.

1. ....
2. ....
3. ....
4. ....
5. ....

Date:

How does this affirmation make you feel?

....

....

....

....

What blocks/negative beliefs are brought up for you

....

....

....

....

Thinking of each block in turn, now say:

- *Please forgive me*
- *I'm sorry*
- *Thank you*
- *I love you*

Today I am grateful for:

....

....

....

Day 55

Today's Affirmation:

Say this affirmation several times out loud with your hand on your heart looking at yourself in the mirror.

If you prefer to write it down, do that here.

1. ....
2. ....
3. ....
4. ....
5. ....

Date:

How does this affirmation make you feel?

....

....

....

....

What blocks/negative beliefs are brought up for you

....

....

....

....

Thinking of each block in turn, now say:

- *Please forgive me*
- *I'm sorry*
- *Thank you*
- *I love you*

Today I am grateful for:

....

....

....

Day 56

Today's Affirmation:

Say this affirmation several times out loud with your hand on your heart looking at yourself in the mirror.

If you prefer to write it down, do that here.

1. ....
2. ....
3. ....
4. ....
5. ....

Date:

How does this affirmation make you feel?

....

....

....

....

What blocks/negative beliefs are brought up for you

....

....

....

....

Thinking of each block in turn, now say:

- *Please forgive me*
- *I'm sorry*
- *Thank you*
- *I love you*

Today I am grateful for:

....

....

....

Day 57

Today's Affirmation:

Say this affirmation several times out loud with your hand on your heart looking at yourself in the mirror.

If you prefer to write it down, do that here.

1. ....

2. ....

3. ....

4. ....

5. ....

Date:

How does this affirmation make you feel?

....

....

....

....

What blocks/negative beliefs are brought up for you

....

....

....

....

Thinking of each block in turn, now say:

- *Please forgive me*
- *I'm sorry*
- *Thank you*
- *I love you*

Today I am grateful for:

....

....

....

Day 58

Today's Affirmation:

Say this affirmation several times out loud with your hand on your heart looking at yourself in the mirror.

If you prefer to write it down, do that here.

1. ....
2. ....
3. ....
4. ....
5. ....

Date:

How does this affirmation make you feel?

....

....

....

....

What blocks/negative beliefs are brought up for you

....

....

....

....

Thinking of each block in turn, now say:

- *Please forgive me*
- *I'm sorry*
- *Thank you*
- *I love you*

Today I am grateful for:

....

....

....

Day 59

Today's Affirmation:

Say this affirmation several times out loud with your hand on your heart looking at yourself in the mirror.

If you prefer to write it down, do that here.

1. ....
2. ....
3. ....
4. ....
5. ....

Date:

How does this affirmation make you feel?

....

....

....

....

What blocks/negative beliefs are brought up for you

....

....

....

....

Thinking of each block in turn, now say:

- *Please forgive me*
- *I'm sorry*
- *Thank you*
- *I love you*

Today I am grateful for:

....

....

....

Day 60

Today's Affirmation:

Say this affirmation several times out loud with your hand on your heart looking at yourself in the mirror.

If you prefer to write it down, do that here.

1. ....
2. ....
3. ....
4. ....
5. ....

Date:

How does this affirmation make you feel?

....

....

....

....

What blocks/negative beliefs are brought up for you

....

....

....

....

Thinking of each block in turn, now say:

- *Please forgive me*
- *I'm sorry*
- *Thank you*
- *I love you*

Today I am grateful for:

....

....

....

How do I feel my mindset has improved over the last 30 days?

How do I want the Universe to guide me in the next 30 days?

Day 61

Today's Affirmation:

Say this affirmation several times out loud with your hand on your heart looking at yourself in the mirror.

If you prefer to write it down, do that here.

1. ....
2. ....
3. ....
4. ....
5. ....

Date:

How does this affirmation make you feel?

....

....

....

....

What blocks/negative beliefs are brought up for you

....

....

....

....

Thinking of each block in turn, now say:

- *Please forgive me*
- *I'm sorry*
- *Thank you*
- *I love you*

Today I am grateful for:

....

....

....

Day 62

Today's Affirmation:

Say this affirmation several times out loud with your hand on your heart looking at yourself in the mirror.

If you prefer to write it down, do that here.

1. ....
2. ....
3. ....
4. ....
5. ....

Date:

How does this affirmation make you feel?

....

....

....

....

What blocks/negative beliefs are brought up for you

....

....

....

....

Thinking of each block in turn, now say:

- *Please forgive me*
- *I'm sorry*
- *Thank you*
- *I love you*

Today I am grateful for:

....

....

....

Day 63

Today's Affirmation:

Say this affirmation several times out loud with your hand on your heart looking at yourself in the mirror.

If you prefer to write it down, do that here.

1. ....
2. ....
3. ....
4. ....
5. ....

Date:

How does this affirmation make you feel?

....
....
....
....

What blocks/negative beliefs are brought up for you

....
....
....
....

Thinking of each block in turn, now say:

- *Please forgive me*
- *I'm sorry*
- *Thank you*
- *I love you*

Today I am grateful for:

....
....
....

Day 64

Today's Affirmation:

Say this affirmation several times out loud with your hand on your heart looking at yourself in the mirror.

If you prefer to write it down, do that here.

1. ....
2. ....
3. ....
4. ....
5. ....

Date:

How does this affirmation make you feel?

....

....

....

....

What blocks/negative beliefs are brought up for you

....

....

....

....

Thinking of each block in turn, now say:

- *Please forgive me*
- *I'm sorry*
- *Thank you*
- *I love you*

Today I am grateful for:

....

....

....

Day 65

Today's Affirmation:

Say this affirmation several times out loud with your hand on your heart looking at yourself in the mirror.

If you prefer to write it down, do that here.

1. ....
2. ....
3. ....
4. ....
5. ....

Date:

How does this affirmation make you feel?

....

....

....

....

What blocks/negative beliefs are brought up for you

....

....

....

....

Thinking of each block in turn, now say:

- *Please forgive me*
- *I'm sorry*
- *Thank you*
- *I love you*

Today I am grateful for:

....

....

....

Day 66

Today's Affirmation:

Say this affirmation several times out loud with your hand on your heart looking at yourself in the mirror.

If you prefer to write it down, do that here.

1. ....
2. ....
3. ....
4. ....
5. ....

Date:

How does this affirmation make you feel?

....

....

....

....

What blocks/negative beliefs are brought up for you

....

....

....

....

Thinking of each block in turn, now say:

- *Please forgive me*
- *I'm sorry*
- *Thank you*
- *I love you*

Today I am grateful for:

....

....

....

Day 67

Today's Affirmation:

Say this affirmation several times out loud with your hand on your heart looking at yourself in the mirror.

If you prefer to write it down, do that here.

1. ....
2. ....
3. ....
4. ....
5. ....

Date:

How does this affirmation make you feel?

....

....

....

....

What blocks/negative beliefs are brought up for you

....

....

....

....

Thinking of each block in turn, now say:

- *Please forgive me*
- *I'm sorry*
- *Thank you*
- *I love you*

Today I am grateful for:

....

....

....

Day 68

Today's Affirmation:

Say this affirmation several times out loud with your hand on your heart looking at yourself in the mirror.

If you prefer to write it down, do that here.

1. ....

2. ....

3. ....

4. ....

5. ....

Date:

How does this affirmation make you feel?

....

....

....

....

What blocks/negative beliefs are brought up for you

....

....

....

....

Thinking of each block in turn, now say:

- *Please forgive me*
- *I'm sorry*
- *Thank you*
- *I love you*

Today I am grateful for:

....

....

....

Day 69

Today's Affirmation:

Say this affirmation several times out loud with your hand on your heart looking at yourself in the mirror.

If you prefer to write it down, do that here.

1. ....

2. ....

3. ....

4. ....

5. ....

Date:

How does this affirmation make you feel?

....

....

....

....

What blocks/negative beliefs are brought up for you

....

....

....

....

Thinking of each block in turn, now say:

- *Please forgive me*
- *I'm sorry*
- *Thank you*
- *I love you*

Today I am grateful for:

....

....

....

Day 70

Today's Affirmation:

Say this affirmation several times out loud with your hand on your heart looking at yourself in the mirror.

If you prefer to write it down, do that here.

1. ....
2. ....
3. ....
4. ....
5. ....

Date:

How does this affirmation make you feel?

....

....

....

....

What blocks/negative beliefs are brought up for you

....

....

....

....

Thinking of each block in turn, now say:

- *Please forgive me*
- *I'm sorry*
- *Thank you*
- *I love you*

Today I am grateful for:

....

....

....

Day 71

Today's Affirmation:

Say this affirmation several times out loud with your hand on your heart looking at yourself in the mirror.

If you prefer to write it down, do that here.

1. ....
2. ....
3. ....
4. ....
5. ....

Date:

How does this affirmation make you feel?

....

....

....

....

What blocks/negative beliefs are brought up for you

....

....

....

....

Thinking of each block in turn, now say:

- *Please forgive me*
- *I'm sorry*
- *Thank you*
- *I love you*

Today I am grateful for:

....

....

....

Day 72

Today's Affirmation:

Say this affirmation several times out loud with your hand on your heart looking at yourself in the mirror.

If you prefer to write it down, do that here.

1. ....
2. ....
3. ....
4. ....
5. ....

Date:

How does this affirmation make you feel?

....

....

....

....

What blocks/negative beliefs are brought up for you

....

....

....

....

Thinking of each block in turn, now say:

- *Please forgive me*
- *I'm sorry*
- *Thank you*
- *I love you*

Today I am grateful for:

....

....

....

Day 73

Today's Affirmation:

Say this affirmation several times out loud with your hand on your heart looking at yourself in the mirror.

If you prefer to write it down, do that here.

1. ....
2. ....
3. ....
4. ....
5. ....

Date:

How does this affirmation make you feel?

....

....

....

....

What blocks/negative beliefs are brought up for you

....

....

....

....

Thinking of each block in turn, now say:

- *Please forgive me*
- *I'm sorry*
- *Thank you*
- *I love you*

Today I am grateful for:

....

....

....

Day 74

Today's Affirmation:

Say this affirmation several times out loud with your hand on your heart looking at yourself in the mirror.

If you prefer to write it down, do that here.

1. ....
2. ....
3. ....
4. ....
5. ....

Date:

How does this affirmation make you feel?

....

....

....

....

What blocks/negative beliefs are brought up for you

....

....

....

....

Thinking of each block in turn, now say:

- *Please forgive me*
- *I'm sorry*
- *Thank you*
- *I love you*

Today I am grateful for:

....

....

....

Day 75

Today's Affirmation:

Say this affirmation several times out loud with your hand on your heart looking at yourself in the mirror.

If you prefer to write it down, do that here.

1. ....
2. ....
3. ....
4. ....
5. ....

Date:

How does this affirmation make you feel?

....

....

....

....

What blocks/negative beliefs are brought up for you

....

....

....

....

Thinking of each block in turn, now say:

- *Please forgive me*
- *I'm sorry*
- *Thank you*
- *I love you*

Today I am grateful for:

....

....

....

Day 76

Today's Affirmation:

Say this affirmation several times out loud with your hand on your heart looking at yourself in the mirror.

If you prefer to write it down, do that here.

1. ....
2. ....
3. ....
4. ....
5. ....

Date:

How does this affirmation make you feel?

....

....

....

....

What blocks/negative beliefs are brought up for you

....

....

....

....

Thinking of each block in turn, now say:

- *Please forgive me*
- *I'm sorry*
- *Thank you*
- *I love you*

Today I am grateful for:

....

....

....

Day 77

Today's Affirmation:

Say this affirmation several times out loud with your hand on your heart looking at yourself in the mirror.

If you prefer to write it down, do that here.

1. ....
2. ....
3. ....
4. ....
5. ....

Date:

How does this affirmation make you feel?

....

....

....

....

What blocks/negative beliefs are brought up for you

....

....

....

....

Thinking of each block in turn, now say:

- *Please forgive me*
- *I'm sorry*
- *Thank you*
- *I love you*

Today I am grateful for:

....

....

....

Day 78

Today's Affirmation:

Say this affirmation several times out loud with your hand on your heart looking at yourself in the mirror.

If you prefer to write it down, do that here.

1. ....
2. ....
3. ....
4. ....
5. ....

Date:

How does this affirmation make you feel?

....

....

....

....

What blocks/negative beliefs are brought up for you

....

....

....

....

Thinking of each block in turn, now say:

- *Please forgive me*
- *I'm sorry*
- *Thank you*
- *I love you*

Today I am grateful for:

....

....

....

Day 79

Today's Affirmation:

Say this affirmation several times out loud with your hand on your heart looking at yourself in the mirror.

If you prefer to write it down, do that here.

1. ....
2. ....
3. ....
4. ....
5. ....

Date:

How does this affirmation make you feel?

....

....

....

....

What blocks/negative beliefs are brought up for you

....

....

....

....

Thinking of each block in turn, now say:

- *Please forgive me*
- *I'm sorry*
- *Thank you*
- *I love you*

Today I am grateful for:

....

....

....

Day 80

Today's Affirmation:

Say this affirmation several times out loud with your hand on your heart looking at yourself in the mirror.

If you prefer to write it down, do that here.

1. ....

2. ....

3. ....

4. ....

5. ....

Date:

How does this affirmation make you feel?

....

....

....

....

What blocks/negative beliefs are brought up for you

....

....

....

....

Thinking of each block in turn, now say:

- *Please forgive me*
- *I'm sorry*
- *Thank you*
- *I love you*

Today I am grateful for:

....

....

....

Day 81

Today's Affirmation:

Say this affirmation several times out loud with your hand on your heart looking at yourself in the mirror.

If you prefer to write it down, do that here.

1. ....
2. ....
3. ....
4. ....
5. ....

Date:

How does this affirmation make you feel?

....

....

....

....

What blocks/negative beliefs are brought up for you

....

....

....

....

Thinking of each block in turn, now say:

- *Please forgive me*
- *I'm sorry*
- *Thank you*
- *I love you*

Today I am grateful for:

....

....

....

Day 82

Today's Affirmation:

Say this affirmation several times out loud with your hand on your heart looking at yourself in the mirror.

If you prefer to write it down, do that here.

1. ....
2. ....
3. ....
4. ....
5. ....

Date:

How does this affirmation make you feel?

....

....

....

....

What blocks/negative beliefs are brought up for you

....

....

....

....

Thinking of each block in turn, now say:

- *Please forgive me*
- *I'm sorry*
- *Thank you*
- *I love you*

Today I am grateful for:

....

....

....

Day 83

Today's Affirmation:

Say this affirmation several times out loud with your hand on your heart looking at yourself in the mirror.

If you prefer to write it down, do that here.

1. ....
2. ....
3. ....
4. ....
5. ....

Date:

How does this affirmation make you feel?

....

....

....

....

What blocks/negative beliefs are brought up for you

....

....

....

....

Thinking of each block in turn, now say:

- *Please forgive me*
- *I'm sorry*
- *Thank you*
- *I love you*

Today I am grateful for:

....

....

....

Day 84

Today's Affirmation:

Say this affirmation several times out loud with your hand on your heart looking at yourself in the mirror.

If you prefer to write it down, do that here.

1. ....
2. ....
3. ....
4. ....
5. ....

Date:

How does this affirmation make you feel?

....

....

....

....

What blocks/negative beliefs are brought up for you

....

....

....

....

Thinking of each block in turn, now say:

- *Please forgive me*
- *I'm sorry*
- *Thank you*
- *I love you*

Today I am grateful for:

....

....

....

Day 85

Today's Affirmation:

Say this affirmation several times out loud with your hand on your heart looking at yourself in the mirror.

If you prefer to write it down, do that here.

1. ....

2. ....

3. ....

4. ....

5. ....

Date:

How does this affirmation make you feel?

....

....

....

....

What blocks/negative beliefs are brought up for you

....

....

....

....

Thinking of each block in turn, now say:

- *Please forgive me*
- *I'm sorry*
- *Thank you*
- *I love you*

Today I am grateful for:

....

....

....

Day 86

Today's Affirmation:

Say this affirmation several times out loud with your hand on your heart looking at yourself in the mirror.

If you prefer to write it down, do that here.

1. ....

2. ....

3. ....

4. ....

5. ....

Date:

How does this affirmation make you feel?

....

....

....

....

What blocks/negative beliefs are brought up for you

....

....

....

....

Thinking of each block in turn, now say:

- *Please forgive me*
- *I'm sorry*
- *Thank you*
- *I love you*

Today I am grateful for:

....

....

....

Day 87

Today's Affirmation:

Say this affirmation several times out loud with your hand on your
heart looking at yourself in the mirror.

If you prefer to write it down, do that here.

1. ....
2. ....
3. ....
4. ....
5. ....

Date:

How does this affirmation make you feel?

....

....

....

....

What blocks/negative beliefs are brought up for you

....

....

....

....

Thinking of each block in turn, now say:

- *Please forgive me*
- *I'm sorry*
- *Thank you*
- *I love you*

Today I am grateful for:

....

....

....

Day 88

Today's Affirmation:

Say this affirmation several times out loud with your hand on your heart looking at yourself in the mirror.

If you prefer to write it down, do that here.

1. ....
2. ....
3. ....
4. ....
5. ....

Date:

How does this affirmation make you feel?

....

....

....

....

What blocks/negative beliefs are brought up for you

....

....

....

....

Thinking of each block in turn, now say:

- *Please forgive me*
- *I'm sorry*
- *Thank you*
- *I love you*

Today I am grateful for:

....

....

....

Day 89

Today's Affirmation:

Say this affirmation several times out loud with your hand on your heart looking at yourself in the mirror.

If you prefer to write it down, do that here.

1. ....

2. ....

3. ....

4. ....

5. ....

Date:

How does this affirmation make you feel?

....

....

....

....

What blocks/negative beliefs are brought up for you

....

....

....

....

Thinking of each block in turn, now say:

- *Please forgive me*
- *I'm sorry*
- *Thank you*
- *I love you*

Today I am grateful for:

....

....

....

Day 90

Today's Affirmation:

Say this affirmation several times out loud with your hand on your heart looking at yourself in the mirror.

If you prefer to write it down, do that here.

1. ....
2. ....
3. ....
4. ....
5. ....

Date:

How does this affirmation make you feel?

....

....

....

....

What blocks/negative beliefs are brought up for you

....

....

....

....

Thinking of each block in turn, now say:

- *Please forgive me*
- *I'm sorry*
- *Thank you*
- *I love you*

Today I am grateful for:

....

....

....

How do I feel my mindset has improved over the last 30 days?

What areas do I feel I still need to work on?

The Runner's Success Affirmations to choose from:

I am a runner

※ ∞ ※ ∞ ※

I believe in myself

※ ∞ ※ ∞ ※

I believe I can

※ ∞ ※ ∞ ※

I believe in my abilities

※ ∞ ※ ∞ ※

I am a confident runner

※ ∞ ※ ∞ ※

I will achieve my goals

※ ∞ ※ ∞ ※

I will perform at my best

※ ∞ ※ ∞ ※

I am confident in my abilities

※ ∞ ※ ∞ ※

I will succeed

※ ∞ ※ ∞ ※

My mind and body are strong

※ ∞ ※ ∞ ※

My body performs as I ask it to

※ ∞ ※ ∞ ※

I am calm and composed

I can do it

※ ∞ ※ ∞ ※

I've got this

※ ∞ ※ ∞ ※

I trust my training

※ ∞ ※ ∞ ※

I am proud of my achievements

※ ∞ ※ ∞ ※

I love to learn and improve

※ ∞ ※ ∞ ※

I am growing mentally and physically stronger each day

※ ∞ ※ ∞ ※

I treat my body well

※ ∞ ※ ∞ ※

I take care of myself

※ ∞ ※ ∞ ※

I stick to my plan

※ ∞ ※ ∞ ※

I rise up stronger from setbacks

※ ∞ ※ ∞ ※

I am learning and growing all the time

※ ∞ ※ ∞ ※

I am open to opportunities

I grow in confidence everyday

※ ∞ ※ ∞ ※

My self-belief is high

※ ∞ ※ ∞ ※

I know I can

※ ∞ ※ ∞ ※

I am a dedicated runner

※ ∞ ※ ∞ ※

I take good care of myself

※ ∞ ※ ∞ ※

I make wise training decisions

※ ∞ ※ ∞ ※

I balance training and recovery

※ ∞ ※ ∞ ※

I heal stronger

※ ∞ ※ ∞ ※

I heal well

※ ∞ ※ ∞ ※

I will come back stronger

※ ∞ ※ ∞ ※

I dream it and then I do it

※ ∞ ※ ∞ ※

My mind is focused on achieving my goal

※ ∞ ※ ∞ ※

I focus on my strengths

※ ∞ ※ ∞ ※

I am passionate about my running and it shows in everything I do

※ ∞ ※ ∞ ※

I am fearless

※ ∞ ※ ∞ ※

I love challenges, they bring out the best in me

※ ∞ ※ ∞ ※

I deserve my dreams

※ ∞ ※ ∞ ※

I am overflowing with achievement

※ ∞ ※ ∞ ※

I am worthy of success in my running and life

※ ∞ ※ ∞ ※

I excel in all that I do

※ ∞ ※ ∞ ※

I am constantly improving

※ ∞ ※ ∞ ※

I train with passion, purpose, and confidence

※ ∞ ※ ∞ ※

I believe in myself and my abilities

※ ∞ ※ ∞ ※

No matter what comes my way, I can do it

※ ∞ ※ ∞ ※

I am unstoppable

※ ∞ ※ ∞ ※

I am enough

※ ∞ ※ ∞ ※

I am capable

※ ∞ ※ ∞ ※

I love what I do

※ ∞ ※ ∞ ※

I can be at my best

※ ∞ ※ ∞ ※

I can achieve my dreams

※ ∞ ※ ∞ ※

I deserve this

※ ∞ ※ ∞ ※

I grow stronger every day

※ ∞ ※ ∞ ※

I am a strong and confident competitor

※ ∞ ※ ∞ ※

My mind is free of resistance

※ ∞ ※ ∞ ※

I can do anything I set my mind to

※ ∞ ※ ∞ ※

I can step outside of my comfort zone and succeed

※ ∞ ※ ∞ ※

I train, I learn, I grow

※ ∞ ※ ∞ ※

I am in complete control

※ ∞ ※ ∞ ※

I now release the past and move on to my new goals

※ ∞ ※ ∞ ※

Achieving my goals is getting easier and easier

※ ∞ ※ ∞ ※

I have a clear plan of action to achieve my goals

※ ∞ ※ ∞ ※

Recovery is training

※ ∞ ※ ∞ ※

I meet my body's needs so I can run at my best

※ ∞ ※ ∞ ※

I'm still a runner even when I'm not running

※ ∞ ※ ∞ ※

I am motivated at all times to train

※ ∞ ※ ∞ ※

I am becoming more focused by the day

※ ∞ ※ ∞ ※

Motivation comes naturally to me

※ ∞ ※ ∞ ※

I find it easy to stay focused

※ ∞ ※ ∞ ※

Positive thinking comes easily to me

※ ∞ ※ ∞ ※

I keep on pushing myself

※ ∞ ※ ∞ ※

I set goals and reach them

※ ∞ ※ ∞ ※

I was born to do this

※ ∞ ※ ∞ ※

Nothing can stop me

※ ∞ ※ ∞ ※

I am a great athlete

※ ∞ ※ ∞ ※

I am a fierce competitor

※ ∞ ※ ∞ ※

I am a winner

※ ∞ ※ ∞ ※

I am naturally driven to achieve my goal

※ ∞ ※ ∞ ※

I think more positively each day

※ ∞ ※ ∞ ※

I am a positive thinker

※ ∞ ※ ∞ ※

I always push myself

※ ∞ ※ ∞ ※

I find it easy to stay motivated

※ ∞ ※ ∞ ※

I always work hard

※ ∞ ※ ∞ ※

I have great stamina

※ ∞ ※ ∞ ※

I am dedicated to my training

※ ∞ ※ ∞ ※

I am motivated to run

※ ∞ ※ ∞ ※

I am a skilled runner

※ ∞ ※ ∞ ※

I am growing more confident each day

※ ∞ ※ ∞ ※

I stay focused under pressure

※ ∞ ※ ∞ ※

I am improving my form

I thrive under pressure

※ ∞ ※ ∞ ※

I am in the zone

※ ∞ ※ ∞ ※

Focusing comes easily

※ ∞ ※ ∞ ※

I am recognised for my abilities

※ ∞ ※ ∞ ※

I enjoy running more and more each day

※ ∞ ※ ∞ ※

I train consistently

※ ∞ ※ ∞ ※

I am becoming a great runner

※ ∞ ※ ∞ ※

I will reach my full running potential

※ ∞ ※ ∞ ※

My stamina is increasing

※ ∞ ※ ∞ ※

I perform at my best

※ ∞ ※ ∞ ※

I am learning to love training

※ ∞ ※ ∞ ※

I am becoming a positive thinker

※ ∞ ※ ∞ ※

I am becoming more motivated by the day

※ ∞ ※ ∞ ※

I naturally think positive thoughts

※ ∞ ※ ∞ ※

I naturally take action to support my running

※ ∞ ※ ∞ ※

Motivation is a normal part of my everyday life

※ ∞ ※ ∞ ※

My stamina is naturally high

※ ∞ ※ ∞ ※

Focusing my mind is something I naturally do

※ ∞ ※ ∞ ※

I can reach any running goals that I want

※ ∞ ※ ∞ ※

My endurance is high

※ ∞ ※ ∞ ※

My running abilities are naturally strong

※ ∞ ※ ∞ ※

Running regularly is fun

※ ∞ ※ ∞ ※

I enjoy running

※ ∞ ※ ∞ ※

Staying motivated at all times is easy for me

Running is something I love to do

※ ∞ ※ ∞ ※

I stick to my training schedule

※ ∞ ※ ∞ ※

I am becoming fitter and fitter

※ ∞ ※ ∞ ※

I have a clear mind

※ ∞ ※ ∞ ※

I am confident in my abilities

※ ∞ ※ ∞ ※

I have excellent rhythm

※ ∞ ※ ∞ ※

I am physically strong

※ ∞ ※ ∞ ※

I have incredible endurance

※ ∞ ※ ∞ ※

I have a winning mindset

※ ∞ ※ ∞ ※

I am dedicated to training in all its forms

※ ∞ ※ ∞ ※

My confidence is high

※ ∞ ※ ∞ ※

I have a growth mindset

※ ∞ ※ ∞ ※

My form is good

※ ∞ ※ ∞ ※

I find it very easy to think positively

※ ∞ ※ ∞ ※

*I always make sure to push myself in my
training sessions*

※ ∞ ※ ∞ ※

I can stay focused under pressure

※ ∞ ※ ∞ ※

I have the skills needed to run well

※ ∞ ※ ∞ ※

I perform well in my events

※ ∞ ※ ∞ ※

I am mentally strong

※ ∞ ※ ∞ ※

I can stay positive throughout competition

※ ∞ ※ ∞ ※

I like the challenge of competition

※ ∞ ※ ∞ ※

I am in charge of how I feel

※ ∞ ※ ∞ ※

I can and I will

※ ∞ ※ ∞ ※

It's my time

I choose to perform with a focused mind

※ ∞ ※ ∞ ※

I have unlimited potential

※ ∞ ※ ∞ ※

I learn from all my performances

※ ∞ ※ ∞ ※

My ability to persevere is limitless

※ ∞ ※ ∞ ※

I am a champion

※ ∞ ※ ∞ ※

I am an unstoppable force

※ ∞ ※ ∞ ※

I am a success

※ ∞ ※ ∞ ※

I was made to do this

※ ∞ ※ ∞ ※

I am able

※ ∞ ※ ∞ ※

I run to the best of my abilities each day

※ ∞ ※ ∞ ※

I am completely focused on my goal

※ ∞ ※ ∞ ※

I am dedicated and excited to practice

※ ∞ ※ ∞ ※

I am a strong competitor

※ ∞ ※ ∞ ※

I have amazing stamina

※ ∞ ※ ∞ ※

I am committed to my training

※ ∞ ※ ∞ ※

I am a highly skilled runner

※ ∞ ※ ∞ ※

I perform my best under pressure

※ ∞ ※ ∞ ※

I am turning into a great runner

※ ∞ ※ ∞ ※

*Through practice I will achieve my full
running potential*

※ ∞ ※ ∞ ※

My stamina is constantly increasing

※ ∞ ※ ∞ ※

*Every day I am becoming stronger and
stronger*

※ ∞ ※ ∞ ※

I always enjoy the training process

※ ∞ ※ ∞ ※

*I naturally focus my mind when I need to
concentrate*

※ ∞ ※ ∞ ※

I enjoy training hard

※ ∞ ※ ∞ ※

I naturally achieve all my running goals through hard work

※ ∞ ※ ∞ ※

I naturally have strong running abilities

※ ∞ ※ ∞ ※

Motivation is easy for me to find when training

※ ∞ ※ ∞ ※

I have a high level of endurance

※ ∞ ※ ∞ ※

Running comes naturally to me

※ ∞ ※ ∞ ※

I exceed my expectations

※ ∞ ※ ∞ ※

I push myself

※ ∞ ※ ∞ ※

I always perform my best

※ ∞ ※ ∞ ※

I can reach any goal

※ ∞ ※ ∞ ※

Meeting my goals is the best feeling in the world

※ ∞ ※ ∞ ※

I set high goals for myself

※ ∞ ※ ∞ ※

I'm cool, positive and confident

※ ∞ ※ ∞ ※

I stay relaxed and in control at all times

※ ∞ ※ ∞ ※

I focus all my energy on the job at hand

※ ∞ ※ ∞ ※

Michelle Griffiths-Reeve

Michelle is the founder of The Runner's Therapist and is an accredited CBT (cognitive behavioural therapy) and EMDR (eye movement desensitisation and reprocessing) therapist, sports NLP practitioner, certified mindset coach, as well as a dedicated runner.

Michelle offers a unique combination of therapy and mindset coaching to runners who struggle with underlying mental health difficulties and find themselves developing an unhealthy relationship with their sport. She is passionate about helping runners to run from a place of good mental health and confidence, whilst loving every step and in the right mindset to perform at their best!

Having spent over 19 years working in the mental health service, Michelle has dedicated her career to helping people develop and maintain mental wellbeing, confidence and happiness so they can achieve their dreams, both in running and in life.

Contact Michelle:
https://therunnerstherapist.co.uk/
https://www.facebook.com/therapyforrunners
https://www.instagram.com/therunnerstherapist

Jo Outram

Jo is a Certified Mindset Coach, primarily working with women in business to improve their wealth (abundance). She is the author of a number of mindset and affirmation journals, helping develop positive mindsets in areas such as wealth, self-love, love and business success.

Contact Jo:
www.jooutram.com
www.instagramcom/mindset_upgrade_tools

Printed in Great Britain
by Amazon

72341539R00129